W9-CKM-470

Sara Swan Miller

Ants, Bees, and Wasps of North America

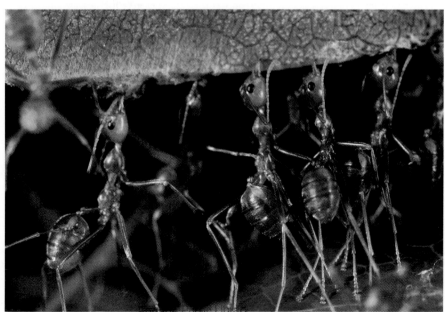

Franklin Watts - A Division of Scholastic Inc.
New York • Toronto • London • Auckland • Sydney
Mexico City • New Delhi • Hong Kong

Photographs © 2002: Animals Animals: 5 top right, 29 (Patti Murray), 15 (James H. Robinson), 21 (Allen Blake Sheldon); Dembinsky Photo Assoc.: cover (Thomas C. Boyden), 41 (E.R. Degginger), 25 (Gary Meszaros); Edward S. Ross: 19; Minden Pictures/Mark Moffett: 1; Photo Researchers, NY: 42 (Scott Camazine), 6 (Lynwood M. Chace), 27 (E.R. Degginger), 39 (Jacana), 5 bottom right (Karl Maslowski), 13 (Stephen P. Parker), 17, 31 (J.H. Robinson), 37, 43 (Kenneth H. Thomas); Robert & Linda Mitchell: 7; Visuals Unlimited: 23 (Joe McDonald), 33 (Janine Pestel), 5 top left (Robert C. Simpson), 5 bottom left (Ken Wagner), 35 (R. Williamson).

Illustrations by Pedro Julio Gonzalez, Steve Savage, and A. Natacha Pimentel C.

The photo on the cover shows a bee collecting nectar. The photo on the title page shows a colony of weaver ants repairing a nest.

Library of Congress Cataloging-in-Publication Data

Miller, Sara Swan.
Ants, bees, and wasps of North America / Sara Swan Miller.
    p. cm. – (Animals in order)
    Summary: Introduces the different animals in the hymenoptera order, their similarities and differences, environments in which they live, and how to observe them.
Includes bibliographical references and index.
    ISBN 0-531-12244-1 (lib. bdg.)   0-531-16658-9 (pbk.)
    1. Ants—Juvenile literature. 2. Bees—Juvenile literature. 3. Wasps—Juvenile literature.
[1. Ants. 2. Bees. 3. Wasps.] I. Title. II. Series.
QL565.2.M56 2003
595.79'097—dc21   2002001731

Contents

Meet the Ants, Bees, Wasps, and Their Kin

Have you ever watched honeybees sipping nectar from flowers? Have you seen big bumblebees bumbling around in the garden? Maybe you have watched hornets or paper wasps flying around their paper nests.

You may have thought that these buzzing, stinging insects could be related. You were right! Scientists place all of these insects in the same group, or *order*, called the hymenoptera (hy-meh-NOP-tur-uh). They have certain things in common that other insects don't share.

There are several other insects in this order that you probably didn't suspect were related. Ants, sawflies, horntails, and ichneumons are all hymenopterans.

On the next page are pictures of four insects. Can you guess what makes them all hymenopterans?

Cow killer

Northern paper wasp

Black carpenter ant

Honeybee

Traits of the Hymenopterans

There are two things that all hymenopterans have in common—their wings and their mouthparts. "Hymenoptera" comes from two Greek words. *Hymen* means "membrane," and *ptera* means "wings." The insects in this order have two pairs of membranous wings, the front ones larger than the hind ones. These wings have large cells and few veins. However, some groups within the order are wingless.

Hymenopterans all have chewing mouthparts that are good for munching on pollen, wood, or other insects. Bees and some wasps also have "tongues" that they use to sip nectar.

Hymenopterans go through several stages before they become adults.

Females of most species have a long egg-layer called an *ovipositor*. In bees, wasps, and some ants the ovipositor has developed into a stinger, which they use to defend themselves and their nests. Only the females in these species have stingers. Other hymenopterans, even though they may look scary, don't sting.

Compare the shape of the wasp and the ant with the shape of the honeybee. Ants and wasps have a thin "waist" called a *pedicel*, between the base of the abdomen and the thorax. Honeybees don't have pedicels.

Like butterflies and moths, hymenopterans go through *complete metamorphosis*. An egg hatches into a *larva*, which feeds for a time before

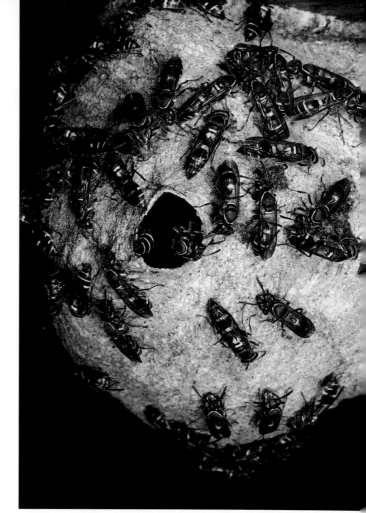

Some members of the hymenoptera order live in large colonies.

resting as a *pupa*. As it pupates, it slowly turns into an adult.

Most hymenopterans are solitary, but several are highly social. The social ones live together in colonies with a single queen and many female workers. The workers are specialized to do different jobs in the colony. Ants, honeybees, paper wasps, and hornets live in societies that are more complex than any other insect society except termites.

The Order of Living Things

A tiger has more in common with a house cat than it does with a daisy. A true bug is more like a butterfly than a jellyfish. Scientists arrange living things into groups based on how they look and how they act. A tiger and a house cat belong to the same group, but a daisy belongs to a different one.

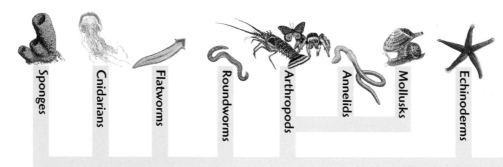

Sponges | Cnidarians | Flatworms | Roundworms | Arthropods | Annelids | Mollusks | Echinoderms

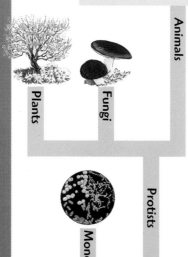

Plants | Fungi | Animals | Protists | Monerans

All living things can be placed in one of five groups called *kingdoms*: the plant kingdom, the animal kingdom, the fungus kingdom, the moneran kingdom, and the protist kingdom. You can probably name many of the creatures in the plant and animal kingdoms. The fungus kingdom includes mushrooms, yeasts, and molds. The moneran and protist kingdoms contain thousands of living things that are too small to see without a microscope.

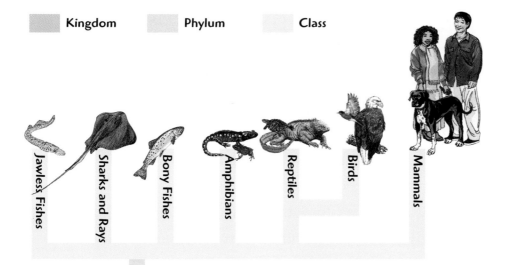

Kingdom   Phylum   Class

Jawless Fishes

Sharks and Rays

Bony Fishes

Amphibians

Reptiles

Birds

Mammals

Chordates

Because there are millions and millions of living things on Earth, some of the members of one kingdom may not seem all that similar. The animal kingdom includes creatures as different as tarantulas and trout, jellyfish and jaguars, salamanders and sparrows, elephants and earthworms.

To show that an elephant is more like a jaguar than an earthworm, scientists further separate the creatures in each kingdom into more specific groups. The animal kingdom can be divided into nine *phyla*. Humans belong to the chordate phylum. All chordates have backbones.

Each phylum can be subdivided into many *classes*. Humans, mice, and elephants all belong to the mammal class. Each class can be further divided into orders; orders into *families*, families into *genera*, and genera into *species*. All the members of a species are very similar.

9

How Hymenopterans Fit In

You can probably guess that hymenopterans belong to the animal kingdom. They have much more in common with spiders and snakes than they do with maple trees and morning glories.

Hymenopterans and other insects belong to the arthropod phylum. All arthropods have a tough outer skin called an *exoskeleton*. Can you guess what other living things are arthropods? Examples include spiders, scorpions, mites, ticks, millipedes, and centipedes. Some arthropods, such as lobsters, crabs, and shrimps, live in the ocean. These arthropods are called crustaceans.

The arthropod phylum can be divided into a number of classes. Hymenopterans belong to the insect class. True bugs, flies, butterflies, and beetles are also insects.

There are thirty different orders of insects. The hymenopterans make up one of these orders. This is a large order, with about 105 different families containing about 280,000 species worldwide. They live on every continent except Antarctica.

Let's get to know some of these wonderful insects better!

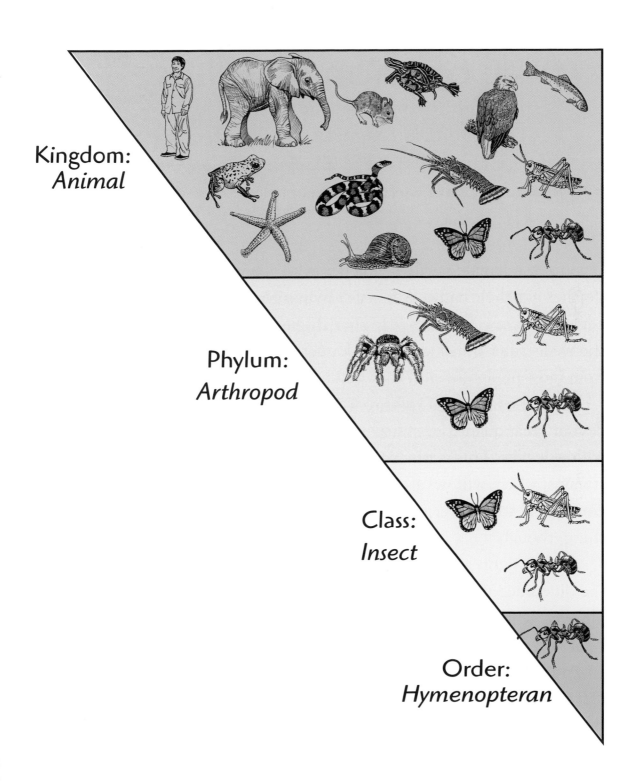

Kingdom:
Animal

Phylum:
Arthropod

Class:
Insect

Order:
Hymenopteran

Common Sawflies

FAMILY: Tenthredinidae
COMMON EXAMPLE: Northeastern sawfly
GENUS AND SPECIES: *Tenthredo originalis*
SIZE: 3/8 inch (9 to 11 mm)

If you saw a female sawfly laying her eggs, you would know how sawflies got their name. A female's ovipositor is long and has toothed edges like a saw. She uses it to slice through the bark of twigs, where she wedges her translucent eggs. Under the bark, the eggs are safe from most predators until they hatch a few weeks later.

Then the larvae get right to work. They have huge appetites and devour great quantities of leaves. Northeastern sawflies prefer to eat willow leaves. This is why you are most likely to see the larvae near streams, where willows grow best. A large group of feeding larvae can completely strip a tree of its leaves. Adult sawflies eat hardly anything, though.

At first sight, sawfly larvae look like caterpillars, but you can tell the difference if you look closely. Sawfly larvae have one pair of simple eyes, while caterpillars have six pairs. Caterpillars have little hooks on their *prolegs*, but sawfly larvae have no hooks.

Another way to tell whether you're looking at sawfly larvae or caterpillars is to watch how they position themselves on a leaf. Sawfly larvae usually feed with their tails hanging downward off the leaf. Caterpillars usually keep all of themselves on top of the leaf.

You might guess that sawflies can be real pests, since they can do such damage to trees. But one species, Ucona acaenae, can be beneficial. It was brought from Chile to New Zealand to control the spreading of a dangerous weed called *Acaena*, which was taking over fields.

Horntails

FAMILY: *Siricidae*
COMMON EXAMPLE: Pigeon horntail
GENUS AND SPECIES: *Tremex columba*
SIZE: 1 to 1 1/2 inches (25 to 38 mm)

Horntails are named for the horny, spearlike plates on their tails. Like sawflies, the larvae can do a lot of damage to trees. Pigeon horntail larvae are particularly fond of elm, beech, oak, maple, and some other hardwood trees.

A female has a long ovipositor that is about a quarter of the length of her whole body. She uses it to bore into a tree and lay a single egg inside. She covers each egg with *fungal spores* that come from a sac in her abdomen. A fungal spore is somewhat like a seed. It will grow into a *fungus*. The fungi attack the wood and soften it. When the eggs hatch, the larvae tunnel easily through the rotting wood, munching as they go. Meanwhile, the fungi keep spreading in the tunnels the larvae make and eventually can kill the tree.

The larvae tunnel inside the tree for two years, devouring the wood and spreading the fungi. Finally, they spin a cocoon of silk and sawdust and pupate just under the bark. A few weeks later, adults emerge from large holes they bore through the bark.

Adult horntails don't feed on wood. They fly from flower to flower, feeding on water and flower nectar.

If you look at maples, beeches, and other hardwood trees in the

fall, you might see dead female horntails hanging from the trunks. After females lay their last eggs, they often die with their ovipositors still stuck in the trees.

Ichneumons

FAMILY: Ichneumonidae
COMMON EXAMPLE: Giant ichneumon
GENUS AND SPECIES: *Megarhyssa macrurus*
SIZE: 1 to 3 inches (25 to 75 mm)

A giant ichneumon is one of the scariest-looking insects you'll ever see. The female is 3 inches (75 mm) long, and has an incredibly long, sharp spear on her tail. It looks as if she could give you a horrible sting. That spear isn't a stinger, but a very long ovipositor. An ichneumon is completely harmless—unless you're a horntail.

After a female mates in the spring, she flies from tree to tree, searching for horntail larvae that are buried inside. She has very long antennae, which she presses against the bark to pick up vibrations. Then, when she "hears" a horntail larva munching inside, she gets ready to lay an egg in its tunnel. She curves her ovipositor up over her abdomen and drills into the bark. The sharp tip cuts deep into the wood until it reaches a horntail tunnel, where the female ichneumon lays a single slender egg.

When the ichneumon larva hatches, it attacks the horntail larva in its tunnel. The ichneumon doesn't gobble up the horntail all at once, though. At first, it eats the less important parts of the horntail larva, which means that the horntail will stay alive for a time. When the ichneumon larva is ready to pupate, it moves in for the kill. It eats the rest of the horntail and then pupates inside its remains.

There are thousands of species of ichneumons around the world. All of their larvae feed on the larvae of other insects or spiders. They help keep the populations of horntails, moths, and other species from getting out of control.

Gall Wasps

FAMILY: Cynipidae
COMMON EXAMPLE: California oak gall wasp
GENUS AND SPECIES: *Andricus californicus*
SIZE: 1/8 to 1/4 inch (3 to 5 mm)

Have you ever seen a lightweight ball about the size of a tennis ball on an oak twig? Did you wonder what it was doing there? That ball was a *gall* that was created when a tiny female gall wasp laid her eggs on the twig.

When a California oak gall wasp lays her eggs on an oak twig, the newly hatched larvae tunnel inward. They inject saliva into the twig, which defends itself by growing a round gall around the larvae. The larvae live inside in separate chambers, where the gall gives them both food and lodging. They are safely hidden from birds and other predators while they eat the spongy tissues inside the twig.

The gall is green at first and gradually turns brown. One of these galls may grow to be 4 inches (10 cm) across! Just before the larvae pupate, they dig an escape tunnel. Then, when fall comes, the adults come flying out of the gall.

There are about six hundred species of gall wasps in North America. Different species lay their eggs on different parts of different trees. Scientists can tell them apart by looking at the galls they cause.

People used to use old galls to make ink. They ground the galls

into powder and boiled them in water with certain chemicals. They used the ink to write with quill pens and, later, with fountain pens.

Ants

FAMILY: Formicidae
COMMON EXAMPLE: Black carpenter ant
GENUS AND SPECIES: *Camponotus
    pennsylvanicus*
SIZE: 1/4 to 1/2 inch (6 to 12 mm)

Out in the woods, an old log lies on the forest floor. From the outside, it looks as if nothing much is going on. But if you could look inside, you would see hundreds of black carpenter ants hard at work. They are busy tunneling through the damp wood with their strong jaws. They are creating a network of tunnels and chambers in which they will live and raise their young.

Despite what many people think, carpenter ants don't actually eat wood, as termites do. Unlike termites, ants don't have special bacteria in their guts that can digest the wood. Carpenter ants have to go outside the nest to find food. Sometimes they eat smaller insects, but mostly they live off fruit juices, honeydew, and other sweets.

Like other ants, carpenter ants live in large, complex colonies. There is one large queen who does all the egg laying and as many as three thousand workers. All the workers have special jobs. Some take care of the eggs, larvae, and pupae in the nest, some guard the nest from intruders, some dig out the nest, and others go off in search of food to bring back to the rest.

All the workers are females that hatch from the queen ant's eggs.

The workers are sterile—they can't mate and lay eggs. They are so closely related that an ant colony can be thought of as one single creature. When intruders attack, single ants will fight them off and often sacrifice themselves for the sake of the whole colony. For ants, the survival of the whole is much more important than the life of a single individual.

Ants

FAMILY: Formicidae
COMMON EXAMPLE: Texas leafcutting ant
GENUS AND SPECIES: *Atta texana*
SIZE: 1/16 to 1/2 inch (1.5 to 13 mm)

What is that little ant doing carrying that big piece of leaf? It must weigh at least ten times as much as the ant weighs! If you had the patience to watch the ant for a few of hours, you would see her lug her load all the way to her nest and drag it inside.

Leafcutting ants don't eat the leaves or needles they collect. Instead, they use them as compost on which the fungus they eat grows. Smaller workers that live inside the nest chew the pieces of leaves into tiny bits and make compost piles. Then they bring pieces of fungus from other piles to live off the ground-up leaves in the new piles. Other workers collect the fungus in their *crop,* which are sacs located in their throats. Then they carry it to the larvae and throw it up for them to feed on. Other workers feed the queen.

As in other ant colonies, all the workers are sterile females. But when spring is on the way, some of the newly hatched larvae will grow wings and become fertile. They fly out of the nest and mate in the air. The males die, but the females go off to start their own nests, each one carrying a little piece of fungus.

A newly mated female bites off her wings and begins digging in the soil. She makes a small nest. Then she puts the pellet of fungus

inside and fertilizes it with her own waste. She feeds it to the larvae that hatch. Once the larvae have grown into workers, they take over the job of enlarging the nest, tending the new larvae, gathering leaves, and growing the fungus for all their younger sisters.

23

Sphecid Wasps
FAMILY: Sphecidae
COMMON EXAMPLE: Cicada killer
GENUS AND SPECIES: *Sphecius speciosus*
SIZE: 1 1/8 to 1 5/8 inches (30 to 40 mm)

It's not hard to guess how cicada killers got their name. The females hunt *cicadas* to feed to their larvae. Cicada killers come out of the ground in August, when cicadas are buzzing in the trees.

The males come out first and begin defending territories. Each one drives other males out of his air space. When a female digs her way out a few weeks later, the male who owns the territory mates with her.

After she mates, the female sets to work digging a burrow. She has shovel-like mandibles and large legs that are good for digging. On her back legs are spurs that help her kick dirt out of the burrow. The burrow may be several feet deep, with many branches and cells. Once her burrow is ready, she lays eggs in each of the cells.

When the larvae hatch, the female flies off to find a cicada. She paralyzes her prey with her stinger, grabs it, flies it down to her nest, and drags it inside. Each larva will have its own cicada to feed on.

Male wasps usually die soon after mating, but not male cicada killers. Males stay nearby and defend their nests, flying at anything that comes near them. It's scary to be chased by a male cicada killer, but he won't hurt you. He doesn't even have a stinger.

Bees

FAMILY: Anthophoridae
COMMON EXAMPLE: Eastern carpenter bee
GENUS AND SPECIES: *Xylocopa virginica*
SIZE: 3/4 to 1 inch (20 to 25 mm)

Spring has come, and the carpenter bees have dug their way out of their winter holes. Several males have discovered a wooden porch that would make a good nest site. Now they are fighting over their territory. They zip and dive around the porch, madly chasing each other. Every so often, one male attacks another in midair. They wrestle and fall to the ground, still clutching each other. People living in the house are scared of these fierce-looking insects zooming about. Is it safe to go out on the porch?

It might seem hard to believe, but male carpenter bees are completely harmless. They have no stinger, and they aren't interested in people. They have eyes only for each other and for the females that soon arrive.

After carpenter bees mate, everything settles down. Each female drills a perfectly round tunnel, about 3/8 inch (1 cm) in diameter, into the wood under the porch railing. The tunnel may be a foot deep. Then the female makes a series of cells, one after the other. She places a ball of pollen in each cell before laying a single egg inside. Safe in their tunnel, the larvae live off the food their mother left them.

In late summer, the larvae pupate and turn into adults. They're ready to fly off, but they have to wait their turn. The bees near the opening of the tunnel go first, with the others all waiting in line.

People often mistake these big bees for bumblebees, with their yellow *thorax* and black abdomens. But a bumblebee is furry, while a carpenter bee's abdomen is shiny.

Velvet Ants

FAMILY: *Mutillidae*
COMMON EXAMPLE: Cow killer
GENUS AND SPECIES: *Dasymutilla occidentalis*
SIZE: 5/8 to 1 inch (15 to 25 mm)

Can a cow killer really kill a cow? Not really, but its sting is so painful that people say it could. A female cow killer can deliver one of the most painful stings of any insect.

The cow killer is one member of a family called velvet ants. Velvet ants aren't actually ants at all, but furry wasps. They are not as narrow-waisted as true ants, and their antennae don't have joints, as ants' do.

Male cow killers have wings, but the females don't. Being wingless actually helps the females get around. They spend much of their time searching for prey underground, and wings would just get in the way. At mating time, a male swoops down, picks up a female, and mates with her in midair.

The mated female then goes searching for bumblebee nests in the ground. She lays one egg beside each *brood chamber* in a bumblebee nest. When the larvae hatch, they get inside the brood chambers and feed on the bumblebee larvae. Finally, the cow killer larvae pupate in the bumblebee larvae's brood chambers.

There are more than 450 species of velvet ants in North America, found mostly in the Southwest. Most of them lay their eggs in the

30

nests of ground-nesting wasps and bees, including the nests of cicada killers. Many species are brightly colored—red and black, orange and black, or white and black. Those colors are a warning to other animals: Stay away! We sting!

Scoliid Wasps

FAMILY: Scoliidae
COMMON EXAMPLE: Digger wasp
GENUS AND SPECIES: *Scolia dubia*
SIZE: 1/2 to 3/4 inch (13 to 18 mm)

It's spring again, and male and female digger wasps are getting ready to mate. Swarms of them fly low over the ground in figure-eight patterns. It takes days for them to sort themselves out and finally locate mates. Soon after, mated females scamper over the ground, trying to find June beetle larvae hiding below.

When a female digger wasp senses a larva, she starts digging down to find it. She may have to tunnel for several feet. When she finds a larva at last, she stings it and paralyzes it. Once the larva is still, she lays a single egg on it. When the wasp larva hatches, it will have plenty to eat. The paralyzed beetle larva lives for a long time, while the wasp larva slowly consumes it.

People like having digger wasps around. They hardly ever sting people, and they do a great job of controlling June beetles, which can do a lot of damage. Adult June beetles feed on leaves, sometimes destroying a bush. The larvae live underground, feeding on the roots of grasses and other crops, including corn, grain, and potatoes. These larvae may spend up to three years underground, munching away. Be grateful that there are digger wasps to keep the June beetle population under control!

There are several other wasps in the scoliid family. All of their larvae feed on the larvae of different kinds of beetles, most of which are destructive pests in the garden.

The digger wasp is sometimes called the blue-winged wasp. Take a look at its picture to see why.

Bees

FAMILY: Megachilidae
COMMON EXAMPLE: Faithful leafcutter bee
GENUS AND SPECIES: *Megachile fidelis*
SIZE: 3/8 to 1/2 inch (10 to 12 mm)

Have you ever seen a bee flying along with a piece of leaf in its mouth? Did you think it was a honeybee acting strangely? A leafcutter bee and a honeybee are about the same size and look almost the same, but they are different species with very different habits.

Female leafcutter bees work together, cutting round pieces of leaves to line the cells in their nests. With their sharp mandibles, they can snip off pieces of leaves in less than a minute. They dig a tunnel in the ground or inside a rotting log and construct a series of cells. After lining a cell with leaves, the bees stock it with pollen. Then a female lays a single egg inside each cell and seals it shut.

With that pantry of pollen, the larvae grow quickly. They pupate over the winter in their cells. When a larva becomes a mature adult, it has to wait for the others in its nest to mature, too. The young leafcutter bee can't get out of the tunnel until all the ones ahead of it have matured and flown off.

In some ways, though, leafcutter bees are similar to honeybees. The adults feed on nectar. As they fly from flower to flower, they help pollinate plants. Instead of the pollen baskets on their legs that honeybees use to carry pollen, leafcutter bees have pollen brushes under their abdomens that sweep up the pollen. Faithful leafcutter bees especially like daisies, yarrow, asters, sunflowers, and other similar flowers.

Vespid Wasps

FAMILY: Vespidae
COMMON EXAMPLE: Northern paper wasp
GENUS AND SPECIES: *Polistes fuscatus*
SIZE: 1/2 to 1 inch (13 to 25 mm)

As the spring sun warms the earth, a queen paper wasp comes out from under the loose bark where she has spent the winter. She flies off in search of a good nest site. Finally, she decides on the doorway of a nearby house.

She uses chewed-up wood mixed with saliva to construct her paper nest. She creates a thin stalk that hangs down from the top of the doorframe and then begins building six-sided cells attached to the stalk. By the time she is done, she has created an umbrella-shaped nest with several brood cells protected underneath.

The queen lays a single egg in each cell she formed. When the larvae hatch, the queen flies off to hunt caterpillars and other insects to feed them. She doesn't feed her larvae whole insects, though. She chews the prey into little bits first. She herself feeds on nectar.

Finally, the larvae pupate and turn into workers. Now it's their turn to enlarge the nest, take care of the larvae, and take care of the queen. Her only job from now on is to lay more eggs.

In late summer, some of the adults that emerge will be fertile males and females. Off they fly on their mating flight. The males

die after mating, but the females find sheltered places under loose bark or fallen leaves to hibernate.

Paper wasps look scary, but they are usually peaceful. Even if the door next to their nest keeps opening and closing, they will rarely sting—unless you touch the nest!

Ants

FAMILY: Formicidae
COMMON EXAMPLE: Honey ant
GENUS AND SPECIES: *Myrmecocystus navajo*
SIZE: 1/4 to 5/8 inch (5 to 16 mm)

The honey ants of the Southwestern deserts have an odd way of storing their food. They use some of the workers as storage pots! These specialized workers, called *repletes*, spend their whole lives hanging from the ceiling of the underground nest, holding on with their feet. Other workers fill them up with nectar and honeydew they have collected. When members of the colony are hungry, they visit the repletes, which throw up food droplets for them.

The repletes may live as long as ten years, acting as living storage vessels. Sometimes the repletes get overfilled and actually burst open. When this happens, the workers simply glue them back together with sticky silk and saliva. Being a replete certainly doesn't sound like fun!

Like some other species of ants, honey ants tend *aphids* as if they were dairy cows. The aphids squirt sweet honeydew from their tails, which the honey ants lap right up. The ants protect the aphids from predators and even herd them from plant to plant.

Some of the workers are foragers that go off in search of new food supplies. Like other ants, they communicate with one another with their antennae to share news of a new food source. As they trek to

and from the nest, ants lay down trails of formic acid. The scent of the acid leaves a path that other workers can follow to find food and to get back to the nest.

Honey ants are a popular food for many digging mammals, which dig up the nests and eat the repletes. Even humans sometimes eat honey ants!

Vespid Wasps
FAMILY: Vespidae
COMMON EXAMPLE: Potter wasp
GENUS AND SPECIES: *Eumenes fraternus*
SIZE: 5/8 to 3/4 inch (15 to 20 mm)

A potter wasp's nest is small, but you can't mistake it for any other insect's nest. Potter wasps' nests look like little clay pots. You may see them hanging from a window frame, under a porch, or from a tree branch. Each female makes her own pots from mud and lays a single egg in each one. Unlike many wasps, potter wasps live alone.

After making her clay nest, a female attaches an egg inside the wall. Then she flies off to find caterpillars and sawfly larvae to store inside. She paralyzes each one with her stinger and carries it to the nest to feed a larva when it hatches. After she's done stocking the nest, she plugs the hole in the bottom with a pellet of mud.

A female potter wasp usually makes several nest pots. You may see a whole line of them on a branch or under a porch roof. Unlike many other wasps, female potter wasps don't stay around to guard their nests or care for their young. A newly hatched potter wasp larva is completely on its own. But it has plenty to eat, and it is safe inside the clay pot. Birds and other predators can't get at it, and the pot is completely waterproof. Once it has matured, the little wasp makes a hole in the pot and flies away.

Potter wasps buzzing about on the back porch may scare you, but

since they don't guard their nests, they rarely sting. It's actually a good thing to have them around. The larvae feed on insect pests, and the adults pollinate plants as they fly about, sipping nectar.

Watching Hymenopterans

Lots of people enjoy bird watching, but how would you like to start a new hobby? You could be a hymenopteran watcher! Hymenopterans are everywhere.

Spring and summer are the best times to look for bees. In the early spring, they visit tree flowers. In the summer, you can find bees in flower gardens, meadows, and even vegetable gardens. When you set off to look for hymenopterans, take along a field guide of insects and another on flowers. Bring a notebook and pen to write down what you see.

Follow a bee through a garden and observe what flowers it lands on.

If you find bees in a flower garden, pick a single bee and watch it. How many flowers does she visit before she flies back to the hive? Does she visit different kinds of flowers, or the same kind? What kind of flower is her favorite? Usually, honeybees visit only one species of flower at a particular time of the season. This is what makes them such good pollinators, because the right pollen winds up on the right flower.

Spring is a good time to look for paper wasps and hornets building their paper nests. Take along your insect field guide and your notebook and pen. Look under the eaves of buildings, under a porch railing, or on tree branches out in the woods. Don't get too close, though! Hornets have very painful

Try to find a hymenopteran working on its nest and write down what you observe.

stings. When you do find a nest, write down what you find. How big is the nest? What shape is it? Can you tell what species you're looking at by referring to your field guide? Do you see a single wasp working on the nest or several of them? If you see only one, that's a queen just starting her new nest.

Watching ants is easy. They are everywhere, even in city parks. Look on the ground for anthills. Do you see the worker ants "talking" to each other with their antennae? Do the ants groom their antennae with their feet? They need to keep the antennae free of dust, so that they can feel and smell with them. Pick a single ant to watch and follow her. How far does she go? Does she find food? What kind? What else do you notice? Write down what you find out and draw pictures, if you like.

Be on the lookout for other kinds of hymenopterans too. There are more than seventeen thousand species of hymenopterans in North America. That gives you plenty of them to look for!

Words to Know

aphid—a tiny insect with a sucking mouth that feeds on plant juices

brood chamber—an area inside an insect's nest in which the larvae develop

cicada—an insect with sucking mouthparts that feeds on plant juices

class—a group of creatures within a phylum that share certain characteristics

complete metamorphosis—the name for the growth stages of insects that go from egg, to larva, to pupa, to adult

crop—a sac inside an insect's body in which it stores food

exoskeleton—the hard outer covering of arthropods

family—a group of creatures within an order that share certain characteristics

fungal spore—a tiny, seedlike ball that will grow into a fungus

fungus—a primitive plant that feeds on rotting matter or acts as a parasite

gall—a growth on a plant that develops when certain insect species lay their eggs in the plant tissue

genus (plural **genera**)—a group of creatures within a family that share certain characteristics

kingdom—one of the five divisions into which all living things are placed: the animal kingdom, the plant kingdom, the fungus kingdom, the moneran kingdom, and the protist kingdom

larva (plural **larvae**)—the first stage of an insect's development after it hatches from an egg

mandible—the chewing mouthparts of some insects

order—a group of creatures within a class that share certain characteristics

ovipositor—a female insect's egg layer

pedicel—a thin stalk that connects the thorax and the abdomen of wasps, bees, and ants

phylum (plural **phyla**)—a group of creatures within a kingdom that share certain characteristics

proleg—a false leg on the abdomen of a caterpillar that disappears after it pupates

pupa (plural **pupae**)—a stage in an insect's development during which it changes from a larva to an adult

replete—a worker honey ant that is used as a storage jar for honey

species—a group of creatures within a genus that share certain characteristics. Members of a species can mate and produce young.

thorax—the second section of an insect's body, just behind the head

Learning More

Books

Brimmer, Larry Dane. *Bees (True Books–Animals)*. Danbury, CT: Children's Press, 2000.

Facklam, Margery. *What's the Buzz? The Secret Lives of Bees (Rain Forest Pilot)*. New York: Raintree Steck-Vaughn, 2000.

Julivert, Angels. *The Fascinating World of Ants*. Hauppauge, NY: Barrons Juveniles, 1991.

Pascoe, Elaine. *Ants (Nature Close-Up)*. Woodbridge, CT: Blackbirch Press, 1998.

Robinson, W. Wright. *How Insects Build Their Amazing Homes (Animal Architects)*. Woodbridge, CT: Blackbirch Press, 1999.

Steele, Christy. *Ants (Animals of the Rain Forest)*. New York: Raintree Steck-Vaughn, 2000.

Video

Tell Me Why: Insects. Vision Quest Video.

Web Sites

The Bug Club Page has a list of insect experts that you can contact by e-mail. The club also organizes local field trips and publishes a newsletter six times a year.
http://www.ex.ac.uk/bugclub

Insecta Inspecta World has all kinds of information about insects, including hymenopterans.
http://www.insecta-inspecta.com

Index

Meet the Author

Sara Swan Miller has worked with children all her life, first as a Montessori nursery-school teacher and later as an outdoor environmental educator at the Mohonk Preserve in New Paltz, NY. As director of the preserve school program, Miller has led hundreds of schoolchildren on field trips and taught them the importance of appreciating and respecting the natural world, including its less lovable "creepy-crawlies."

Miller has written a number of children's books, including *Three Stories You Can Read to Your Dog*; *Three Stories You Can Read to Your Cat*; *Three More Stories You Can Read to Your Dog*; *Three More Stories You Can Read to Your Cat*; *What's in the Woods? An Outdoor Activity Book*; *Oh, Cats of Camp Rabbitbone*; *Piggy in the Parlor and Other Tales*; *Better than TV*; and *Will You Sting Me? Will You Bite? The Truth About Some Scary-Looking Insects*. She has also written several books on farm animals for the Children's Press True Books series, a set of books on strange fishes, amphibians, reptiles, birds, and mammals for the Watts Library, and several other books in the Animals in Order series.